PRAISE FOR *County of Kings*
Written and performed by Lemon Andersen
Directed and developed by Elise Thoron

"Mr. Andersen has a distinctive talent that makes words sing in ways that insist you listen." —*New York Times*

"In compelling and well-performed iambics, whose artfulness somehow takes the hurt out of the horror, Andersen evokes and enacts the barbarous Brooklyn of his youth."
—*New Yorker*

"The language in Andersen's show is so much fun that it's tempting to quote the entire script, but probably best not to. You can't read his thick, old-school Brooklyn accent or his slightly nervous-looking gaze, and those are the things that make his oddly precise turns of phrase ring out like punchlines." —*Variety*

"The show is a fast-moving, lyrical ode to the unforgiving stomping grounds where he came of age—Kings County, N.Y., better known as Brooklyn. In a masterful blend of verse, rap and dialogue, Andersen paints a highly original portrait of his beloved urban wonderland, capturing both its bleakness and brilliance." —*Associated Press*

"Andersen has a prodigious gift for language, making words arc and soar, and conjuring unexpected rhymes."
—*Village Voice*

"Andersen infuses the evening with a humor and self-awareness that alleviates its grimness. He refuses to present himself as a victim, making his rags-to-not-quite-riches tale all the more inspirational." —*New York Post*

"This is the real-life tale of a kid whose hard-knock life led him to pick up the pen and eventually get on stage. Not to become a rapper, but to become a hip-hop poet."
—*XXL.com*

"Lemon Andersen's *C* ⋯s
through all the many
livering a brutally ho
story to the times as

D0830297

COUNTY OF
KINGS

LEMON ANDERSEN

COUNTY OF KINGS
PUBLISHING

Developed and directed for the stage by Elise Thoron

•   •   •

Copyright © 2009 Lemon Andersen
Front cover photo by Najlah Feanny
Editorial and production consultant: Paola Soto

County of Kings is published by County of Kings Publishing
c/o 190 Marcy Avenue 17F, Brooklyn, New York 11211

ISBN: 0-9761401-0-1
ISBN13: 978-0-9761401-0-8

Designed by Claudia Martinez

First Printing: November 2009
Second Printing: October 2010
Third Printing: April 2012
Fourth Printing: July 2013

Manufactured in the United States of America

To purchase additional copies of this book, or for general information,
contact: countyofkingspublishing@gmail.com or call (646) 701-1492.

Dedicated to the most honorable Wynn Handman.

Table of Contents

WATCH
ME

WATCH me and my 1983 bop gee,
New York City's son
of LQ's, Union Square, and The Roxy's
watch how these *American Idol* Simons
try to stop me
hate me when I walk through the door
love me when I blow up the spot
pleeease
when they first see me they never take me serious
till they find out my talent don't come
from the color of my skin
but from my whole hearted experience.

So watch me
me and my story how I lived it
if you was my mother every morning
I would be walking you to the Methadone Clinic.

My older brother's in Iraq killing corner store Arabs
America I don't forgive it.
So watch me deal with the ridicule and shame
the worst heartache and pain and how I maintained
is by turning myself into the king
of the poetry spit fame.

Now watch me turn my pennies into dimes
my darkness into shine
many of my mistakes into nailing it forever one time
watch me make love to hard work ethics
'cause game without ambition is game never respected
these are not words,
these are my blood sweat and tears
from the real side of Franklin County
to them Sunset Park piers
and my homies in the prison yard still finishing they years
cause I'm an ex-con
but an ex-con has always been a friend to me
don't discriminate 'cause it was written
that even Jesus had a felony.

So watch me be an artist who was born ready made,
watch me take my lemons
and make the best goddamn lemonade.

T h e
TON Y S

WOULD you look at that? Wow, there are so many people out there. After all the hard work I'm finally here—the Tony Awards. When they say this is the great white way, man they sure aren't playing. Either they put some extra lighting out there, or there is a whole lot of white people in that audience. Some artists suffer from stage fright; I suffer from not being on stage enough.

Ok, they're rounding us all up stage left and we get into our huddle. Steve Colman plays the hype-man, and yells, "Def Poets what time is it?" We all holler back, "It's time to get live, it's time to represent."

They announce the award for our category in Special Theatrical Event. I'm thinking, *Ah shiiit, here we go with the word special again.*

Special ed . . .
Ooh you're so special.
In a special case like yours . . .
Today we have a special on special needs.
Isn't that special?

"Yessss!!" We run out on stage giving each other daps and hugs. They're passing the award around and it finally comes to me. I stare at the chromed out Antoinette Perry coin with glory and think to myself, *Damn, this is real. I won.* I wish I can say a couple of words but I look over into the orchestra pit and I can see an old violinist with a permanent hickey on his neck getting ready to play right after Russell speaks. Well whatever, I made it and now I am ready to shut down Times Square where they are live broadcasting another moment for us spit kings to rock the Tonys.

We get to the location. Metal cranes are swinging over-sized video cameras around a stage set in front of the George M. Cohan statue. I jump on stage and the cast all smile at me. Being the only performer out of the whole show born and raised in this city, and in all the prayers we had before the show this is the one thing I'd always asked for. Tonight the police barricades are all over Times Square. Traffic has stopped just so I can tell my story in TV timing.

A BEAUTIFUL
STRUGGLE

I am in the heart of it all
behind this city
there is a history of struggle
a beautiful struggle
these are my streets
my stories

How did I end up here?

NATIVE
NEW YORKER

STARING down the fly famed fashion district of
   Seventh Avenue
looking left to the school trips I took to Rockefeller Center
On my right, the famous arcade I played hooky at
now sells eggnog lattes during the winter
I'm two miles away from the greatest hangout, the old
   Unique Boutique
where my Village people shopped, stomped, and housed
   their way
through Washington Square's cold benches
I can still smell the glazed Yips rib tips, cheap chicken
   fried rice
feeding me on my way
messengering big checks from Goldman Sachs
to the pre-9/11, post car bomb of One World Trade
day dreaming of a Battery Park lifestyle

Instead I have to put up with the punkness
of a Park Slope sucker famed repertoire
Red Hook's school zoned bullying
Even now, the bell tolls from the Yusef Hawkins
aluminum Louisville Slugger
banging against a black Bensonhurst pair of balls
till the sound drops out

My only year in high school
watching the crackle of Abraham Lincoln
splitting a rail
down the line of an All-City Wagner varsity defense

Where off to my first thought
no memory of mine can see further past

    Do you see it?

The sun drenched sight, sound
and sandy flashing lights

    Do you hear it?

That's where it all started
that's where I got it—
Coney Island beach's
Himalaya

HᴵᴹᴬᴸᴬʸA

"Mɪʟʟɪᴇ, it's so hot out today. 'Cause we in Coney Island, can we go to the aquarium?"

Quicker than I could plead, she lets me have it, ghetto Puerto Rican style.

"What? Que tú cre? That I'm made out of money? My God meng, I don't know, que el problema? Tu si que jode. That's why I didn't bring Peter, porque the two of you juntos me vuelven a la super condenao loca. Yo fui a el face-to-face. You know what they pay me? Huh? Los pelos de los panties mio and one hundred dollars en el food stamps and they don't take that at the aquarium, and if you don't like it quedáte con tu pai', because he's a good for nothing blanco desgraciao concho."

Believe it or not she is actually in a good mood. My mother Millie is only five feet full of tough tenderness. A rare proud less Puerto Rican by way of a campo called Cayey. Rigorous, rebellious, reckless one; born second out of seven children. Chosen to sip the chilled chalice of the 1970's tough love supreme, but behind her bold boiling points, she loves me so unconditional.

I say, "Okay Millie, then can we go hangout at the Himalaya ride to dance?"

See, I knew she would say yes. That's the only thing I like about Coney Island in the summer anyway, is the Himalaya. 'Cause the beach is a mess hall of drunk lifeguards getting robbed under the boardwalk, the sand is like walking bare-footed on hot coal. Plus, you have broken glass everywhere.

So finally when she couldn't get no more bronzed, Millie gets up off her floral house blanket, folds it into her red pleather oversized purse and we're off to the Himalaya. I love this ride so much. It would spin around in circles really fast in these up and down waves, then slow down and go backwards on request. The theme around the ride is all these painted mountains of snow with men skiing down the slopes, but it isn't the ride that people love about the Himalaya, it's the music. There's always a party outside and the DJ would play all the latest and classic disco joints. So when me and Millie finally get to the Himalaya it is packed with people from all over the city.

We work our way into the flashy crowd, trying our best to stay on everybody's one, when all of a sudden the DJ plays my mother's favorite record "Ring My Bell." She takes me by the hand, catches a beat, and we start doing our hustle. I look up and see Millie staring at me with those baby brown pearls, swaying a silk scarf tightly wrapped around her Dark-and-Lovely dyed curls. With the layaway jewelry on her prison tattooed arms that she got from the prenda lady. Tempting to lose grip towards the hook. That's when Millie lets go and gives her ten-year-old manchild the solo of his life.

LOOK MA,
I'M DANCING

THIS moment of mine medium rare
so I don't let her down
every shimmy
every shake
every slide
and every glide slides in sync
the crowd tightens their cipher
black folks look at me crooked eye
giving my two-step this get out of town look
it's like no one or nothing else exists
but their soul clap and
the stained glass river Nile of tears
salty, stinging my mother's smile
I could hear her pitch perfect in the background yelling

"That's MY BOY!"

MRS. JUDY

We on the B train heading home and I'm cheezin' the whole ride back. I am reliving that Himalaya soul train moment over and over.

"Hey Millie, can we go back? Did you see all the people looking at me? Especially the lady in the huevo boots."

We get out on the Twenty-fifth Street station and walk a block over to where we live with my half brother Peter and my stepfather, Chado. It stares down at me like Fort Knox, the courtyard, a five floor brick building that stretches on Fourth Avenue, between Twenty-third and Twenty-fourth Street. We live in apartment D5, a two-bedroom on the leaky last floor with a window view that stretches out to the Hudson River. Anchored with parked merchant marine ships, behind the big boats, lighting up the sky with a made-in-France torch, is a tall broad named the Statue of Liberty.

Every family in the courtyard stays here. I guess the parents feel safe with their children's chase for the street life being blocked off by these brick walls. Plus, no child is left unwatched by the old women who are like pigeons with a bird's-eye view on all things gossip.

> *"Ah, shut up, you got a big head and that's all they need to know, you half Puerto Rican, half sports mascot. With a head like that who's your daddy? Mr. Met?"*

That's Mrs. Judy. She's the mayor. She knows everybody's business, and acts like she can only see through one eye.

> *"That's one good eye you wish you had. I see things."*

Don't get her started talking about the hood.

> *"I see there is something more angry than the sound of this ghetto. It's the struggle of these poor people, these poor people living in a rich neighborhood. Lord, that sort of pressure will turn you into a seven-thirty."*

Which, if you don't know, is the hospital term for the criminally insane.

"And the holidays was the worst. There sure ain't nothing holy 'bout them holidays. They just remind us more and more of what we ain't got. Like this blonde boy Andy and his brillo-haired brother Peter, their momma Millie is always sick for the holidays, and they'd be made fun of for not wearing new tennis shoes and sharing each other's pants. I don't understand why these kids in the ghetto make fun of other kids in the ghetto. If you ask me, the way I see it, it's all the same project, and I only got one eye. Ah, there go Choo-Choo with his book bag again, waiting for Peter to come down so they can go train tracking. Hey Choo, that bag should be filled with books instead of all that flat-black you stole from R&S Strauss, and next time I go to the store they better be some deodorant sticks. Damn boys be robbing all up the roll-on, stuffing 'em with shoe Griffin, and topping them with chalkboard erasers, making them homemade markers. I might be blind but I ain't stupid, stupid. I know you going down into them train tunnels. Remember the last time you went down there with your cousin Coco? He came back looking like a burnt biscuit."

Wow, Mrs. Judy is letting Choo have it. Millie rushes upstairs to the crib, but I sit on the front stoop and watch Mrs. Judy burn Choo-Choo. My brother Peter comes down the stairs with a bag full of tools to vandal the walls and trains with. Now, as you can see, we don't look alike. I mean, he's dark skin, I'm white; he got black hair, mine is light. We have different fathers, same mother, same blood type. And I'm like, "Yo, what is up big bro? I see you off bombin' that's def. Can I go?" And he's like,

> *"No, you're a toy, and boy you're going to be wasting up all my ink on your wack-ass letters."*

He brushes me off and heads out the courtyard and bombin' with Choo-Choo.

ME AND MY
BIG BRO

BOY'EE I would do anything to hang out with Peter
even though I don't look like him
I am still his little brother
if he had a tag
I was little to his everything
like if he was Rock
I was Little Rock
if he was Man
I was Little Man
Stan, I was Little Stan
damn, I'm his biggest fan
and he don't understand
that he is my favorite homeboy forever
the Run to my DMC
the Michael Jackson to my pleather

Although we fistfight till midnight

over peanut butter blankets
granted, he was more bolder, more older
Millie would take his ass and spank it
and even though he had it coming
I would stand there with a bloody nose running, fronting
telling my mother it wasn't Peter

"Millie, I wasn't looking. I ran into something."

'Cause he was the black sheep
and I was always referred to as her golden child
Oliver Twist kid with a Kool-Aid smile

My big bro
was whom everybody cursed
caught playing hooky
caught stealing from the purse
neither the baby
nor the first
and when you are the in-between child
you always got it the worst
then he had to share everything with me
from his He-Man underwear
to his tight BVDs
to his only two pair of dungarees

"Big bro, please
I just want to spend time with you."

But he rather go out bombing graffiti on the wall with RAE, rest in peace, Mike D, and Choo-Choo.

FIVE FLIGHTS
UP

I walk five flights up
and I'm rockin' to the beat
five flights
make me so light on my feet

FOUR flights up
    and I'm heading to my home
    four flights
    helps me keep a pace to my pizoem

        THREE flights up
            till sancocho for the soul
            three flights
            gives me more breath control

            TWO flights up
                to the crib of imagination
                this is how I got humility and patience

                LAST floor, we're here
                    the tenement of the trenches
                    welcome to apartment D5
                    where I learned to lose my mind
                    and gain my senses

MILLIE IS
SLEEPING

OPEN the door. "Shh. Be vewy, vewy quiet. Millie is sleep-ing, so we gotta play vewy vewy quietly." She always takes naps at the weirdest time. I'm glad today she can sleep in the bed, 'cause usually she falls out in the middle of talking while she's standing up. I mean she would be wide awake one second, and then next thing you know she's knocked out standing up. All of her best friends at Coffey Park would do the same thing, so I guess it's normal. The funny thing is that I put five dollars down that they never fall down.

Ah anyway, I'm glad I didn't go with Peter bombing 'cause they're about to give my favorite show on TV, *American Bandstand*. So once I get this coat hanger bent in the right way, there goes Dick Clark introducing, no wait a minute, it's Andy Gibb! Andy Gibb is singing on *American Band-stand*. How many of you guys know who Andy Gibb is? Man,

county of kings

you guys are old. Andy Gibb is the hippest white boy in the world. He makes me believe that my Yankee ass could have some soul. Ah, that's the joint.

Come on, come with me to the secret place in the house where I karaoke it like a Korean champ—the bathroom mirror. First, you got to jump on top of the sink and begin by blowing facial expressions and all, till the song ends and you take the famous Andy Gibb bow.

Whoa, I see something behind the toilet. Yes, it's my Lone Ranger belt. Check this out, my stepfather, Chado does this right before he chases me around the house snapping his belt. Oh cool I see something else, one of those syringey things I don't like getting shot with at the doctor's. Alright, this will make a great sword for my Voltron toy, and it shoots water too, that's dope B. I gotta show Millie.

"Millie wake up. Look, watch this. C'mon, I want to show you something. You fell asleep again with a cigarette in your hand. You see? The last time you almost burnt the crib down. You need to stop using your cup as an ashtray 'cause we're running out of good cups to drink juice out of . . . . What's that in your mouth? Ah, get up, you didn't even finish your lunch . . . . Get up! Boy, you are out cold. You don't look good. Alright, I'm gonna get Cookie."

COOOKIEEE!

F. A. G.
Free and Gorgeous

"*Ah please little child, I am more of a man than you can ever be, more of a woman than you can ever handle*"

Cookie, I'm ten years old. I'm not supposed to know all that.

"*Pero papi, one day you gonna have to learn to live life, honey.*"

Well, no, doi! Right now I don't care.

"*Ay, I need to lose weight and these tetas don't look good together. Why couldn't they make them uneven like a real woman?*"

Dag, stop bugging yo, for real B'. If my friends find out you here, then I'ma get ranked on. Can you just help me get this? It looks like there's like a vienna sausage in Millie's mouth?

"*Ay, Papi, that's not a vienna sausage. Your mother is swallowing her tongue!*"

A whole episode of *The Bloodhound Gang* passes before the ambulance comes and pulls Millie out of apartment D5 on a stretcher.

FIVE FLIGHTS
DOWN

FIVE flights down
I don't know what's going on
five flights down
something whispers in my ear
"Child, you gotta stay strong"

FOUR flights down
Millie's out on a stretcher
four flights down
me and my frown
but lucky I got my red Etch-A-Sketcher

THREE flights
my neighbor Rose is holding her
pink nosed pit bull
there's tension in the air, the dog drools
stares at the cop who got his hand on his pistol

TWO flights
too much to see
so many people from the courtyard
with they hands on they heart
and they eyes on me

LAST floor down I could still hear
Cookie upstairs crying so loud
and the silence of the MC in the struggle
moving the crowd

CHA**D**O

THE EMS guys ask me who's my guardian, and before he can call BCW, my stepfather Chado shows up yelling, "Dat's me!"

See, that's my stepfather Chado. He's a self-made thug. Right out of Bayamon, black camel hair goateed with a slim, trimmed jail build. After two years of being with my real father Pete, Millie got tired of trying out the kinder punk side of love. She couldn't lie to herself anymore. My mother likes that pulling hair, gnashing of the teeth, "y mandandote pal' carajo" type of love. So when she met Chado at the dope spot buying some manteca and Valiums with used car parts, she knew this was the man for her. To tell you the truth, I don't even remember if they dated, 'cause it just seemed like Chado moved in overnight and cared for me and my brother Peter like we were his right and left nut.

Most dads teach their children sports, take 'em to basketball games, fly a kite. But living with Chado, me and Peter were taught the finer things in life, like how to make a pen gun. When defending yourself, you always go for the throat. And, of course, my favorite game of all, how-to-strip-a-car-in-broad-daylight.

Chado is the breadwinner of the family, so whatever he does wrong to society feels right on the dinner table. You crazy. I love waking up and finding car parts in the living room 'cause that means we is going to Chuck E. Cheese's.

Chado always takes me and Peter with him to work. And so while Millie is in the hospital detoxing, Chado takes us to strip cars. Peter doesn't want to go. He rather stay home drawing and reading Thor comic books. Not me, no way. I'm a goonie. So I jump in Chado's Cutlass and we drive over to his favorite spot to steal cars. The Washington Cemetery right under the overpassing F train. There goes his partner in crime, Pito, standing near what seems to be an old, rusted A-Team van. Pito nods at Chado to give him the sign that "bajando" is not in sight, which is their term for the police. Chado then throws his half a broken Armitron wristwatch at me.

"Trucitu, I want you to time me, okay?"

He calls me Trucitu after the Spanish version of Barney's son Bamm-Bamm from *The Flintstones*.

"So here it is Trucivities, first Jou gonna wait till I get to the car, ping. Then jou gonna start the watch, pong. Y de'pues, once I get the traga larga en el ping pong, and get it ong, you don't stop the estop watch till you see the 'em brake light go blinky blinky. S'okay? Bueno canchifle, jou ready papi?"

"I'm ready Chado." So he jumps out of his Cutlass and I set the time at fifteen seconds past the minute. Chado slides the jimmy in between the glass window and the door. I start the timer now. I keep looking up at him juxing the car and back down at the watch. By the time I look up, he is already in the car with the red break light brightly lit. I look back down at the watch and add up time right quick. When his partner Pito jumps in the driver seat right quick. "Pito, man, did you see that? It took him only thirty-five seconds."

"Yeah, Chado is the best. Heez my meng."

"So Pito, why do you and Chado have spots and bruises on your arm?" He doesn't answer me, he just stays focused on following Chado. "Pito, when I grow up, that's what I'm gonna do. When I grow up, I'ma be the best car thief in the world." Pito gives me this hey-yay look.

"What are you funny? No, jou e gonna go to school, 'kay? Let me and your papi do this."

Chado brings the stolen car to his normal chop shop at Mike's Collision. Chado walks into the mechanic's office. Yess! When he comes out, I'm gonna whack-a-mole. With all the tickets I win from ski-ball, I'ma trade 'em in for one of those porcelain clowns and give it to Millie so she can feel better. "Hey Pito, tell him to stop taking so long. Pito, why you running?" Oh snap, it's the cops. They got Chado. He's coming out of the shop with his hands cuffed. "Bad timing bro . . . bad timing." Chado sits in back of the police car which is parked in front of our Cutlass. He turns around to look at me, trying to tell me something through the glass window. Although I can't hear him, I can read his Spanglish lips and he's shaking his head saying,

>"*Tú sabe que tu mai, jour mother, she's going to kill me.*"

And I lip sync back to him, "Don't worry, I won't tell."

GRANDMA
MAMI

GRANDMA Mami is . . .
The true mother of the fam
Spanish Bible in her apron
saucepan in her left hand
bobby pins in her hair
calloused feet
worn Chinese slippers.
There'll be abandoned buildings burning on the block
if some fool tried to diss her
'cause that's Grandma Mami, she's like no other
a full time mom when your mother couldn't be your
    mother

Millie's in the hospital
Chado's in jail
Medicaid covers medicine
but it don't post bail

so now I gotta stay with my Grandma Mami
but that's ivid-okay
next to Millie
she is my favorite girl in the world anyway.
See, she'll flip a leftover meal that will make your stomach
    go *wow*
she'll yell at you for throwing out the last of the rice

"Papa that's pegao."

When we got sick during winters so cold
forget chicken soup
she made sancocho for the soul
she sings me church hymns
passages from old psalms
sleeping in her old palms
waiting for my parents to come get me
Grandma Mami would make this little homie so calm
minutes turn to hours
hours turned into weeks
I miss Chado so much I hate 'em
Grandma Mami says:

"Watch what you speak . . .
that word hate is for the weak."

"But they're not suppose to leave me,
not supposed to leave me alone."

The clocks tick-tockin'
I don't eat, lose weight waiting . . .
I finally hear the door knock-knockin'
Run to the door
go and I unlock it . . .

"Oh, wack!"

It's my uncle Wango, slurring his words
a bottle of 151 in his back pocket
man, I miss my parents so much.

"Grandma Mami, I don't want to be here anymore
watching novellas is driving me crazy,
going to church is a bore."

I miss stripping cars
miss boogie-woogieing every day
I miss Pito's nod
telling Mrs. Judy to go away.

Days pass more . . .
Another knock on the door
but I pay it no mind
more than likely it's my uncle Wango
kissing another bottle of moonshine,

"No I'm not going to let you in
you smell like bad musk.
You stink of mad gin.
You think you mad tough,
but you a has been.
Nobody wants you here.
You aint nothing but a drunk.
Alright, you want to come in?
First you gotta do the truffle shuffle like chunk . . .
Punk . . .
Huh?"

•   •   •

"Millie, Chado!"

My parents are home. "Peter they're back." My parents
are home. I run to the door like a dog meeting up with his
master. "Oh I love you and missed you so much, don't ever
leave again." They try their best to smile but it's flaky. They
both look dazed and confused. They drop their luggage on
to the kitchen room floor. Walk mami and papi to their bed-
room and lock the door behind them. Peter and me pull out
mami's old Singer sewing machine case, push it up against
the door. Both of us take turns standing on the case, trying
our best to listen in.

"What do you hear?"

"Shhhhh man, I'm trying to listen."

"C'mon B, let me get a turn."

"Shut up, yo."

The door finally opens and Chado goes running out and heads outside. Millie comes out of mami's room and her face is swollen red from crying. She gets on her knees and gives us the tight hug we were waiting for all day. She wipes her tears on our shoulders and kisses us all over our forehead and cheeks. I ask her, "What's wrong, Millie?"

Choking back, she says "heh, not-heh, nothing." We hugged Millie as hard as we could, I take a look up and I see mami sitting on her bed crying on papi's shoulder.

"What happened?"

NEWS
BREAK

THIS JUST IN . . .

THERE IS A NEW KILLER IN AMERICA

AIDS

A
FEROCIOUS
FEROCIOUS
FEROCIOUS DISEASE
THAT ATTACKS THE IMMUNE SYSTEM
IS SWEEPING THE COUNTRY
AND THE WORLD

MAINLINE INFECTING
HEROINE ADDICTS
HOMOSEXUAL MEN
HARRY AND THE HENDERSONS
MISS SEPTEMBER 1986
STUDIO 54 OWNER
CAPTAIN KIRK'S SON
NORMAN BATES

HIV

IS NOT LUCK
IT'S MAGIC JOHNSON
FREDDIE MERCURY TEMPERATURE LOW
SO DON'T SWIM IN THE ROCK HUDSON RIVER
EVERYTHING THAT GLITTERS IS NOT GOLD LIBERACE
AND IF YOU CREATE A RAP GROUP AND CALL IT N.W.A
THEN ALL OF THE F THE POLICES WON'T SAVE YOU
AND IF YOUR PARENTS PLAY SCRABBLE WITH NEEDLES AND BELTS
THAN PREPARE FOR THEIR WEALTH IN WEIGHT LOSS
THEIR DIMPLES TO LOOK LIKE POOL TABLE SIDE POCKETS

I AM SUE SIMMONS
EYEWITNESS NEWS

BREAK
BOYZ
N DA
HOOD

THERE is a saying in New York
Manhattan keeps on making it
Brooklyn keeps on taking it
Bronx keeps creating it
Bronx keeps creating it
Bronx keeps creating . . .

Ma ma say
Ma ma sa
Ma ma coosa

South Boogie Down
alpha of the five borough style
the South BX changed the way we handled our
turf wars

pulling off our leather vests, combat boots
chained Harley Davidson wallets
in exchange for the profile Adidas tracksuits
playboy shoes and suede pumas
scuffed from block party battles
every outlaw gang flip-mode their name
into a dance syndicate
the gangs of the seventies
turned into the dancers of the
eighties, called B-boys

F.M.D.
Floor Master Dancing
Filthy Mad Dogs
A.S.D.
All Star Dancing
All Savage Demons
New York City Breakers
Rock Steady Crew
All the big posses on Broadway
under the umbrella of a Zulu Nation
Being fly and hip to this thing called hop

Hip-hop is the hype, be'lee dat
if it wasn't for the boom-box radio
I carried for all the local break boys
if I wasn't assigned the connector of the extension cord to
     the lamppost

for the turntables to mix-master

I would've never learned to raise the bar on style and
    grace

hip hop is a straight razor

on the blade of the axe that cut my teeth into the

Feld Ballet

came to my school

to audition

so I gave them

a six-step into a flip then freeze

opens the door

to the sweatshop couture designed

sprung floor, endless mirrors

of the Feld Ballet school . . .

The Feld Ballet
School is
GANGSTER

MY first day there is great. The Feld school is stuck in the middle of Manhattan's fashion district. Going to the city is a big deal for any of us who are limited to the four brick walls of the courtyard. If you're lucky you got to go to the city once a year and now I'm given the chance to go twice a week. I go to the floor where the Feld is, take a peep in one of the rooms and I think I see Leroy from *Fame*. "Man this is fresh."

In my own school they never pick me for any of the extra curricular activities. They only pick the PTA students to impress their parents and those kids unfortunately have two left feet. The ballet instructor brings us into the changing room where I meet up with a stoker named Akeem from

Gunhill Road in the Bronx. Akeem is in the back putting up his graf tag on hospital IV stickers and sticking them to the lockers. So I step to him. "Yo, homeboy. What you write?"

"I write 'Glass,' they call me Akeem though. What posse you role with?"

"The Courtyard Saints."

"I'm from T.A.T."

The instructor comes in and hands us two tight white shirts and a pair of black underwear he calls trunks. "Put these on they are mandatory." I feel uncomfortable with having to wear these tights, but hey, if it takes me out of school every week and to the heart of the city, then looking like a fairy isn't going to hurt so bad, and plus, who am I to complain? I just got free underwear and a clean white tee.

Ms. Ann the ballet instructor is trying some basic chore-ography with the students and in walks Mr. Feld: a short crew cut, silver haired white man wearing a grey sport jersey, black spandex pants and worn ballet shoes hold-ing a pointer stick in his hand. Mr. Feld walks towards the middle of our circle at a striking pace. He stares each and everyone of us and slowly speaks.

"Children, you have the opportunity to learn

discipline. I don't expect anything less than your
commitment . . . ."

The wild part about Mr. Feld giving this long speech was not once did I fall asleep or even yawn. He is so real in what he's saying. One thing about growing up in the ghetto, it taught you who was frontin' and this man isn't scared by any of us. He looks us straight in the eyes, knowing that if he ever steps foot on my block his wallet would be paying for somebody's Chinese food takeout. After that speech, I look forward to ballet class more than I look forward to going to the city.

'CAUSE when apartment D5 has no heat,
I have ballet routines to keep me warm.
When the lights go off 'cause we can't pay Con Edison
in the darkness of my room,
I leap into a PBS special of *Masterpiece Theatre*.
Rubber bandage my feet to keep a St. Louis Arch.
Nobody at the Feld is mad over little things
like milligrams of methadone,
face-to-face meetings with welfare.
See, in the Feld school when you mess up,
they don't blame your real father for your mistakes.
Everyone seems so . . .
Whachumacalit?

What's that word Mr. Feld uses when he talks about starting the school . . . Driven. Akeem and me make it to the second level class where they mix us up with the rich private school students who are rocking brand new Lee jeans. Now, there is a rumor going around that if you bring in four Lee patches to the local V.I.M. the store will give you a free pair. So Akeem is on the hunt. Just as I am about to put on my black trunks and head to class he tells me,

> *"Hey, hold back and wait for all the students to leave the changing room, so we can check the lockers and rip off some Lee patches."*

I couldn't say no, and I like Lee jeans just as much as
every other B-boy.
I like stylin', profilin', buck-wildin'.
Being so fly, so fresh to def,
keeps a B-boy smiling.
But if I get caught, it's back to
dancing on the block,
lose this new world I love,
lose the style, lose the grace,
but damn I really love hip-hop.
If only Millie could afford me just one pair of those
pin-stripe Lees, instead I wear these fake jeans
everyone on my block
calls "fleas." I would go all day ballet for a pair of
shell top Adidas, but my kicks got four stripes
and everyone calls them "faridas."

Being funky fresh to def has always been my dream.
Forget demi-pleas, I'ma rip these Lee patches off
and go to V.I.M with Akeem.

We end up with twelve patches in total. Except the next time I show up to the Feld school, they never let me in through the front door. Having a pair of Lee jeans ended not being a deal at all. The next month, they went out of style. Then I was cracked on every time I wore 'em.

"'Cause Lees are for fleas!"

NEWS
BREAK 2

GOOD
AFTERNOON,
I AM
ROSEANNA
SCOTTO

THIS
JUST IN,
THERE
IS A
NEW
KILLER
IN AMERICA

AIDS

A
FEROCIOUS
DISEASE
THAT ATTACKS
THE IMMUNE
SYSTEM IS
SWEEPING
THE COUNTRY . . . .

ME and my cousin Joey are sitting in the living room watching *Animaniacs*. While the show's ending and the credits are rolling, a newscaster pops up on the screen to give an emergency news brief. Like a kid with no sense Joey turns to me and says, "Your mother got that." I want to just deck him. I feel like the thing I dread the most, a victim. That night at home, I sit down on my parents' bed and I ask them, "Do you guys have AIDS?"

Chado turns his head to the window and stares out blank towards the streetlights. Millie puts her hand on my head and says,

> "Si, Trucitu . . .
> Mira papi no suffer por mi.
> You got to be strong mi'jo.
> La familia,
> your family is going back to Puerto Rico.
> Eyo cren que la SIDA e un demonio.
> They think that what I have is a demon.

That's why, cuando yo me muero
I don't want you to live with them.
No te pone como los puertoriqueños.
They don't care about people.
They only care about what people think."

"Millie is that the difference between someone being proud
and someone having pride?"

"Ay papi tú y las palabras,
you y eso words tuyo.
Oye me truqui, no suffer por mi.
No cry
be strong papi.
Los dia van a ser malo.
When those days e mucho para ti
y mi enfermeda te cay mal
papi aguantate.
Hold strong to yourself.
Lucha para tu paz,
fight for your peace.
Porque cuando yo no estoy aqui mas na
ju need to have to ponerte duro.
This world e malo con cojones.
So no te pones como un cabronsito,
because I know,
que tú eres un nene bueno.
Pero being a good kid

las gente they think you stupid and weak, ok?
Y algo mas,
no vas a la funeraria mia.
Don't come to my funeral
'cause I don't want you to see me like that,
me entiende?"

"Ok."

Next day I go to school and during our lunch break some of the students in my class get into a rank off. A kid named Vasco stops the dozens to tell us a joke.

"Hey, what do you call a guy in a wheelchair who has H.I.V?"

Quickly and shamefully I say, "what?"

"Roll AIDS"

All the kids laugh and I fake my laugh along with them. Millie starts becoming more outspoken about being sick to our neighbors in the courtyard and of course they tell their kids who happen to be students at my school. So once they find out, the whole P.S. 172 finds out. In the fifth grade, my last year there, most kids avoid me. Their parents warn them not to sit next to me, share their lunch, or even shake my hand.

G o o N

THEN came the
era of the goon,
and I gotta eat
not a lot of sleep
native tongue sound
over house beat
but I'm doing fine
and I'm getting mine
on the cheese line
everybody lying
talking 'bout me
but they can't see
that I'm a goon now
they can't phase me
homie at dawn
foe at noon
misfortune
blood is all maroon

turn freebase
into crack
we turn hip hop
into gangsta rap
chado dies
peter cries
millie cries
peter tries
suicide
special ed kid
look real close
look iron heart
look steel toes
mtv rocked
more videos
and everybody loved
arsenio
vision boards held rank
clear grip tape
brooklyn bridge banks
whole 'nother level
loved heavy metal
king diamond
peter saw the devil
kings county g building
milk and giz is still top billin'
the era of the goon
rusty fork

silver spoon

fresh air fund

was no fun

got to go to camp

with a good heart

come back with a bad one

gotta get a grip

while the going hood

hood is never good

I don't think you should

shouldn't if I could

can't if you won't

could if I can

till my fam scrammed

ran to the motherland

thought a puerto-ric-can

they planned

on another plan

damn fam left me

and my brother man

tough condition

tough love

double de-composition

watch this mona lisa

spit technician

turn me into a menace

now that's my mission

THE
Gutter

LOUIE da Barber's sistah approaches me on our made-up
Jets versus Giants game being played on a cold April stick-
ball street. She is crying the cry I can't cry no more, and
apologizing for a mistake she didn't make. Choking on the
last word of every verse, she done tells me,

> *"Andy, your brother Peter just . . . called and he*
> *needs you to go to the hos . . . hospital. It's your*
> *Millie. Mother. And it's not good."*

What she doesn't know is that it's always not good and I'm
tired. No weight of the world surprises me anymore. It's
actually the bliss. Bliss shocks me on my way to meet the
end. Her fate. The riding. The rumble of a double R train
back to Lutheran hospital with the joys and hopes of . . . .

N O
MORES

No-MORES
No more pity
No more phone operators knowing me
by my first name cause of all the 911 dialing
No more Pentecostal preacher house visits
like if her sickness was a demon
No more dope fiends asking me if my mother got
No more errands, freeloading
door knocking to borrow milk money from our neighbors
No-mores started to be outshined by only-one-mores

Only one more polished hospital floor
baby blue suited nurse
Only one more Ortiz Funeral Home
Only one more rented suit
Only one more chauffeured hearse
Only one more day of suffering
a life I didn't want to live

Only one more dark night
tomorrows will be bright
all-American, and I will finally live like a regular kid
ya dig?

And I thought that would be fact till in between her bedside
and her life support machine lays her last supper she saved
for me. Accented by my favorite full meal chocolate shake
Ensure that suddenly begins to ripple like if I threw a stone
in its lake, and then the rhyme screams . . . .

TO LIVE IS TO
SUFFER

SEEING her so illy ill
Damn on the really real
You don't know the dealy deal
Or the pain I feely feel
Sugar hill, chilly chill
even though Millie Mill
is suffering, a suffering so similar
to little Emmitt Tilly Till
And you don't know the pain I feel
watching hour upon hour
shower upon shower of high-level
shook shake seizures would devour
choking the life from my momma
my beautiful sick flower
It hurt my heart so
to see her fall apart slow
you don't never know

you won't ever know
to mean the world to someone
then you got to let her go

See, when someone pulls the unworn rug
of unconditional love
the cold floor will creak a household thug.

M I L L I E

slap boxes with

G O D

IMAGINATION helps me make sense out of non-sense-lessness. For the forty-eight long hours Millie fights against the sickle's swing on her barbwire lifeline, I don't get why she just doesn't let go. Till I remembered her biggest fear. See, to her pearly gates is for suckers. She'd piss on a street corner paved with gold—knowing Millie she took a sip of milk and honey and spit it in God's face, and they slap boxed for forty-eight hours and every backhand the Lord lays on my mother 'causes her comatose body to convulse ravagely. But she isn't going nowhere, not till she finds out her biggest fear would not be fulfilled.

MILLIE

What is going to happen to my children? I will not find peace in your pasture. As a matter of fact sell my soul to the dark glow for the glory of my boys.

And God says in his mighty tone,

GOD

Lady, you trippin. I'm busy trying to hold down gravity, keep the planets in orbit, settle the seas to keep the mortality rate low down there, and you want me to take time out of my busy schedule to look after two boys? Woman, don't you know by now how things make sense even to me? Those two are cut from a legacy of hardship, which begets struggle, and of course that begets soul, and unless they know how to pimp their souls, there will be no glory. It is written that my way is the highway for the fishermen and that's what you get for naming them Peter and Andrew, brothers.

And this is where Millie kicked God in the ding-ding with her last request.

MILLIE

My Lord, then can I angel my children through their suffering? Can I line up mastery in their lives so that even their flaws are great?

GOD

Very well, but Andy will suffer from his last nerve.

MILLIE

Even though it's not ghetto. I will help him acquire a taste for calming tea.

GOD

But he is sentenced to cry lonely tears.

MILLIE

But we can make it so that he has a permanent smile.

GOD

And out of all talents given when I rolled his dice it landed on him not minding his own business. How would you figure him to make a living?

MILLIE

Selling it to the world.

GOD

And your son Peter, you know he will never ever let go of the hoes.

MILLIE

As long as he can raise his daughters into women, hoes will never matter.

And the Lord finally said,

GOD

Jesus, Mary and Joseph, you got more comebacks than a Chelsea drag queen. Fine! Don't rest, don't peace out. It is on you. There will be no dogs to lick his wounds, rosaries will do nothing but choke his neck. I will not hold down his fort. I will not lay down the law, lay down the word, is my bond so that those people, that gutter, apple rotten, no pot to piss in forgotten. If Andy does something wrong the burden is yours. You take care of him.

INTRO
Act II

ROOTS rights reggae
was our teenage pregnancy music
When the liquor shot sound comes on
I would grab my high school honey, Lily
take her to the dance floor
and sweat out her perm.

simi**Lily**like

OH, you gotta meet my girl Lily like, Millie's not around,
but Lily was so similar to Millie like, Lily would always
speak in simi-Lily-likes like, like, like . . .

"Like, you know I've been through a lot, like,
I see these, like, little girls running around
acting like grown women
dressing like grown men.
My mother would've like beat my ass
like *Mommie Dearest* if she caught me acting like that.
Like the time with my first love,
this boy from the courtyard,
like nobody, like, wanted their parents to
like let their daughters
have anything to do with, like, boys
let alone like those that came out of that building,

'cause it was like the neighborhood New Jack City,
but their was this one boy I like, forget about it,
anyway
for, like, my fourteenth birthday my mother got me
a pair of these construction Timbs I liked
and my father got me, like, a see through beeper
so you know hip-hop, like,
you could look ugly
but clothes make you look like you the shit.
So, like, I go up to Margaritas,
which was like the corner bodega,
with my, like, cousin Semi to show off and act
like I was buying sunflower seeds and a Chick-O-Stick
and, like, we run into the two-three-four boys from the
courtyard
so, like, my cousin Semi's sister
was already like going out with RAE rest in peace,
who was huggin' the corner like a drug dealer with his
homeboy
they called Lemonhead,
who looked like a thugged out Campbell Soup kid,
so, like, next thing you know
like, this lil' whiteboy Puerto-rock
runs up on me like a chain snatcher
and pulls my beeper from my Mudd jeans,
which always made my ass
look like a Dominican before she has kids.
Anyway, like, he didn't want to give me back my beeper

until, like, I gave him the digits, like, my number
so naïve instead of giving him my number
I, like, gave him my virginity.
I mean, like, he had to hold onto my head to like get
it in
but anyway, we will, like get to that later.
My mother didn't like his reputation,
she thought I, like, would catch AIDS
from just kissing him 'cause, like, his mother had it
so I, like, had to break up with him
and then he became my boyfriend again
but, like, only over the phone for like a year,
he would tell me how he had to, like, live with his uncle
'cause, like, there was no where else for him to go,
and like, his mother didn't want him to do that
and like, his uncle liked taking his father and mother's
death money
and spending it on, like, coke all the time
so he had to, like, get a real job at this place
called Goldman Sachs being a messenger
like, down on Wall Street.
Andy, whose gang started growing wild
like stretch marks on a baby momma panty line
and like, he was growing crazy too with them
so one time I was, like, bored
and I wanted to feel like a gangster's girlfriend
and I told him, like, this boy Blue Chip
who had a front tooth like a lapis lazuli

in school grabbed my ass like a manhandle,
and he didn't do anything.
I got so mad at him 'cause, like, no girl
wants to be with a poser.
Until the day he caught Blue Chip
hanging out with his girlfriend holding hands
and they were wearing each other's sneakers
like, who the fuck does that?
Anyway, like, Andy came over and just knocked him
out.
I heard he, like, hit Blue Chip so hard
he was laid out on the floor
still holding his girlfriend's hand.
Andy then stepped to me and was like,

"Don't worry about when I do things as long as I do them
right."

I was like, "That's my man."

He had this natural smell I liked,
he smelled like Lutheran Hospital.
We became really serious when I started
going to his high school at John Jay
which was like a jungle
and we would cut out of our afternoon classes
and sneak into his uncle's house.
By now all my friends have had sex

and I was the last one
so we would, like, experiment
you know, like, dry humping
sharing each other's gum while making out.
Andy, he already had sex
with some trick, bitch, slut,
I don't know her name, fuck her anyway, he was my man!
After all the pushing and pulling
I took my little brother's played out
red and black lumberjack off
and he pulled off his Phillies blunt white tee
and there we were ass-naked.
He had a chest that looked like E.T.'s
I like cried after showing him my titties,
'cause I had, like, a cripple nipple
but then I was gassed to see how much
he liked looking at my body,
and before you know it, like, we finally did it.
His hands were soft like a dishwasher's.
I don't think he ever took some girl's virginity before
and since I never lost mine
we really didn't know what we were doing.
He put both of his hands on top of my head
like he was climbing a rope,
I gripped on to his butt cheeks
that had a birthmark
that looked like the island of Cuba

and, like, it took him a whole video of TLC to finally
get it in,
but when it went in it felt like a sweet burn.
Then he started reggae dancing in me
to make it look like he had skills
and I went along with it like I knew what I was doing
too.
Everything smelled beautiful and innocent
like puppy water,
we left that crib like a honeymoon stay
at the Liberty Inn standard
till the next day like when my mother did the drive by
on him."

W e SSS i d e

NOW I never picked up and read a whole book before, but it's perfect timing. The summer of '93 is out. The days moved slow with the music 'cause of all this Cali love, Snoop D.O. Double G drops *Doggy Style*. The slang twangs with "I Got 5 On It" riffs, and we all want to know, "Where's the Chronic?"

I come across a blued-up-from-the-shoed-up Crip story called *Monster Kody* by Sanyika Shakur. An Indian sat on every page and lost the streets of Bucktown, USA to the alleys of Grape Street and the shermed out rollin' sixties. No one ever told me behind the papier-mâché studio lots of Hollywood was a thick, solid, ready-made real, bullet shell infested strip called Crenshaw, and to the east was guns but to the west was bigger ones. Now, the beauty of this was really getting to the last page. The story didn't matter anymore. The fact that I finished reading a three-hundred-page book is revolutionary, 'cause numbers speak and they say I have to go to jail to finally pick up a book.

So, I celebrate with Louie da Barber sharing a Papa Smurf acid stamp, watching the world in front of us turn three-dimensional. I literally see a seed planted in the ground blossom into a flower and dwindle away in thirty seconds tops, and I think to myself, *wow acid is a hell of a drug*, and when I turned around to tell Louie da Barber I just witnessed the miracle of life, he's hightailing up the block, chasing something that probably isn't even there. And the trip turns twice blue, fish, silk diapers, math to the twelfth power. Heebi-jeebies at a construction site. And I know that doesn't make sense, but like I said, acid is a hell of a drug. Lucky for me I have the keys to his crib where I can go sober up, but like I said, acid is a hell of a drug and the *Monster Kody* story starts unraveling and coming to life right before me.

I exchange my Phat Farm jeans and Hilfiger top for a blue creased Dickie suit, trade in my Air Max Barkleys for a pair of house slippers and some bright white knee-high tube socks. Stare in the mirror at the reflection of a baby gangster and say, "Whad'up, loc?"

The only thing that's missing is the deuce-deuce, fully loaded, hollow tip. I slip it into my hip and it brings the sun out on my "Gangster's Paradise." I walk out, on my way to the mom and pop's spot, a.k.a. the bodega, to buy some Zig-Zags, a.k.a. Bambú paper, and somebody drives by and tries to bang on me.

I roll up on the car with my hand on my waist, ready to peel the cap off this fool, and they have the nerve to roll down the window like their heart pumps Kool-Aid. I put on the stank face ready to show this sucker this is my block. I poke my head in the window and it's my girl Lily's moms talking about,

"Get your ass in the car, right now."

Now if you ever want to sober up from an acid trip, just let somebody's mother tell you off. I get in the back of that car in fear for my life the way she's yelling at me. The aunt who's driving tries her best to tag-team with her sister, but she's a booty-do. You know, she had more fat on her stomach than her booty do. Her small dynamite rants are being upstaged by all the bombs Lily's moms is dropping on me. Even though I have the roscoe on me, I'm not built to be interior decorating the car with the backs of their skulls. But I'm sure she'd shut the fuck up if I flashed it. Did I just get ignorantly ghetto? Me? Never. So I tell Lily's mom everything she wanted to hear.

"You don't want me to be with your daughter?"

"No!"

"Fine. I wasn't with her a long time anyway."

"So?"

"She don't know what love is."

"Whatever . . . ."

"I was her first, so I got mine."

And the next day, at eighteen I get down on one knee and propose to a fifteen-year-old. Lily didn't care 'cause she was like, "That's my man." I wind up for the next six months doing boyfriend shit I'm not used to: holding hands in public, going to baby showers, staying on the phone all night right after I just dropped her off, buying double-hearted rings, giving each other nicknames like Boonki and Fushi, and anniversaries, God, one-week, two-week anniversaries, a month, an anniversary on our first kiss, hickey anniversary.

Then she and her family wants our two-year anniversary to be an event, like a Cuban Quinceñera, and after just losing my job as a messenger for being too ghetto in the elevator, and my uncle kicking me out 'cause he couldn't raise a man-child anymore, I can't support no girl right now. See, if my mother Millie was around she would tell Lily's mom, "Tú quiere un party? Metete e'te dedo y hacete un party con eso." Damn, I guess there is only one other option.

Dope Boy
Fresh

DOPE boy fresh.
Mr. Manager, lookout.
Pusher-man on the street
Momma ain't around, so how else I'm going to eat?
Puts me in his Lexus, plush leather seats, tells me

"Forget food, these crack vials could put Jordans on your
feet."

I take a couple bundles on the humble
a few bombs on the arm
figure selling poison to my neighbors won't do me no harm
and that was the beginning, then it was all about winning
and living like what I'm doing ain't nowhere near sinning
this money is making me devilish and all about self
yeah I'm selling to my man's moms

'cause if she don't get it from me
she gonna get it from someone else.

And I become heartless and Godless,
regardless of what the old folks in my hood thought
so what, I'm selling what killed my mother?
She was her own grown woman
with her own free will, that's not my fault
and you might not like me
but these Nikes make me feel so loved
wonder what happens when I give this hustle
a little more push and a whole lot more shove
probably make Ph.D. loot without having a degree.

My girl's stressing for my time
but what can she do that this paper can't do for me?
Tell her my mind is on that dollar sign, yo
girl, live your life, don't bother mine, sho'
nuff you want time, whoa
love is love, but holler baby wait on line
go tell your mom that your love's losing manners
to this blow mixed with Arm & Hammer
it's the next best living,
and if she don't understand ghetto grammar
tell her the new nine-to-five is
cocaine mixed with baking soda
the new payola,

drawing funds out of packages
the new Crayola.

Her eyes stay bloodshot
from my long nights on the block
praying a lot that I don't get knocked,
or fall blood, braaaaattt, to the gunshot
she can't sleep 'cause of all the mercies,
she mercies me.
I tell her to,

"Just chill, I got something special for our second anniversary."

But it lands on the fifteenth of the month
which means a guaranteed G-stack
so that night I tell her I that I gotta make a run,

"Baby Girl, I'll be's back,"

but she don't believes that
copping to me a please that,

"Like tonight, like, something ain't right.
Like, my heart don't needs that, like, we don't, like,
need money, like, I don't even care.
Like, why don't we just go upstairs?
Like, my father has some beers, like,

I will let you run an iron, straighten the curlers out
my hair.
Like, if I really mean something to you,
then, like, baby don't go nowhere."

Thinking love or the money?
Money or the love?
Should I go straight with my life,
or should I go straight thug?
Love or the money?
Money or the love?
Should I be living like how I'm living
or should I stop pushing 'dem drugs?
Answer: money might always get spent,
but love don't always pay the rent.
So I'm bent on making this dollar,
even though it don't make any cents.

"Like, he never, like, even listen to me that night
he got caught, like, I knew that what we had was
history."

"What pisses me is that I'm in jail, you should hold me
down."

"Like, I'm only sixteen, like, how long am I supposed
to stay around?"

"Yeah, but you're supposed to be all the way in it, you know, to win it."

"Like remember one thing, like, I was always in it, but the love, like, that I wanted, like, you was never, like, really with it."

"Forget you then. I don't even see you being my spouse."

"Like, I never thought, like, I'd be saying it's over, like, let alone in a courthouse."

"So it's over?"

"Like, over."

"Over, over?"

"Like, over, like, over."

"Then let me go back to my cell and cry on my own shoulder."

count TIME

THEY offered me a year
or five years probation
I take the year with no hesitation
I'm not built to be checking in
pissing in a cup, curfews
telling me what I do's
and what I does
where I'm supposed to be
and where I was

Fuck that
I rather do a year
hopefully good time
will get me up early outta here
but man, I gotta make it clear
I ain't about to show these suckers
that my heart pumps fear.

"What you looking at?
Let's take it to the yard.
I ain't no choirboy queer.
I know I only got a year,
but I will spend the rest of my life in here
flinging your ass off the top tier."

Damn, I only gotta do a year
These twenty-five to lifers
are going to try to have me washing
the doo-doo out they Jockeys
I gotta balance my mouth
be bold and not cocky
No Apollo Creed, but all Rocky

An officer comes to the gate to get me and brings me to
another cell for pedigree. In the distance I can see a large
black man, a hard-rock. His hair line looks like it always
has a bad day, his dreaded salt and peppered beard means
he comes from a Five-Percent nation.

H A R D
ROCK

NOW Hard Rock was known
not to take no shit from nobody
and he had the scars to prove it
split purple lips, ears lumped up
permanent pomegranate
above his yellow eyes
and on the side
he had a buck-fifty straight up
that slammed into his taped up, shaped up
1989 blowout, no doubt
but ya see, you don't know
what I'm talking about
'cause I was one of the few
who spoke to Hard Rock
before I came out
that night we broke night
and in the midst of a prison chat

he tells me that,

> "Listen here young Mighty Joe,
> you don't need to come up in this prison no
> more . . . ."

An adolescent down the hall yells out, "Man, Hard Rock, what you lyin' for?"

> "Fuck you . . . listen here young Mighty Joe,
> there is a better place to fight your time.
> Stay away from the colors
> school brown, project blue
> red lines on the floor
> they're there to institutionalize you
> come here, go back, come here, you know?
> You know what they say?
> They say, if the walls could talk. Well, they do
> I put layers and layers and layers of paint and
> stucco and wallpaper
> but they keep speaking to me in these ten dol-
> lar words
> they say, they say, why go home when you got
> three hots and a cot?
> Why think, be, live, outside the box?
> Where in the box you could do nothing,
> nothing wrong, nothing right, can't tell day from
> night, the walls ask me where I want to be, I say

right here with you
two times."

And just like that
Hard Rock went walking through them doors
handcuffed and shackled
making a rhythm out of his chains
and on the other side of his head
you can see the scar
where the doctors used
to cut out a part of his brain.

The haunting of turning up that way—a knothole in the
fence—keeps me up. Staring through the barred windows,
in the distance I can see a hill. Over the hill there is a place
filled with boot camps, morning PTs, no red lines on the
floor, creased greens instead of project blues, runs around
Riker's Island. The warden offers me programming and I
sign up for high impact boot camp. Feels like a punk chess
move from the outside, a sucker's strategy, but after listen-
ing to Hard Rock, I owe it to the choice he should've made.
Plus, it ain't like I got to listen to anyone.

OFFICER
BROWN

"ANDERSEN! Get your suspicious mulatto ass on the floor right now and give me fifty push-ups! And they better be the Bruce Lee kind. Then I want you to run to the corner of the sprung, stick your face in the corner and yell ten times, 'Discipline is a willful obedience to all lawful orders. Respect for authority and self-reliance.' And if you don't end it on 'Sir' every time you say it, I will double up, you goddamn hear me? And when you're done I need you to come back here and do work detail maggot. And you better have them floors polished till Broadway looks like a glass lake. You call those Bruce Lee push-ups? If I would've known you was going to Bruce Leroy those push-ups, I would've told you to kiss my Converse. Get up, listen boy, chin up, everybody else in your platoon is sentenced to this program for violating parole. You on the other hand chose to be here, you chose this program, so with Officer Brown, drill instructor if you give one shit, I will give back two, you hear me? And that's 'Sir, yes, sir.' Now get to the corner of the sprungs and run it."

DISCIPLINE

AFTER two months of boot camp, they stick me back in population to ride out my time. I look weird to the rest of the inmates in my cell block. I know it's because I don't look comfortable being here. I don't care about phone time, I don't care about stacking day room chairs, can't stand the sight of these men wasting their time playing meaningless games of spades, fighting over a television they don't own, killing over a meal they ain't make. Not me. No way. You won't catch me smiling on Riker's Island. I'm fienin' to hold on to my discipline. I'ma pray harder than the inhouse preacher, out read the prison law librarian, keep hospital corners on my bed to feel normal. I'ma lock my cell, sit on a stack of books, and read.

HOW Steve Biko died, so we can write what we like

How Hajj-Malik-Shabazz passed

Now they think twice before they whoop our ass

'Cause of Jackson George, we deserve to see the sky

'Cause if you look real close you could see blood in my eye

I can't rely on the school system, false education they sold
    me

But we can rely on American history, lies my teacher told
    me

Stick my face in them books, 'cause my habits to read by
    force

And behold I will see a pale white horse

'Cause in them books is all the answers that I seek

Wonder why my mother was stronger than my father

Read the Feminine Mystique

You hate The Man but not as much as

You should hate the man that hit your sister

But you don't know real hate,

Til you read Mein Kampf by Adolf Hitler

Y'all don't know the rules of power

Believe me, I'm not convinced

You know white lies, white lies knows

Nicolo Machiavelli Prince

Attica, Attica, Attica

I run into a poem written by a three-time felon about how
his cold heart would bake warm cookies at the sight of see-

ing his first love again.

Damn, wish I could've said that one. Everyday I look out towards the New York city skyline out in the prison yard and count the wake ups till I face the ultimate haiku:

THE worst thing about
doing a bid in prison
is coming back home

Selling KNOWLEDGE

IT stares down at me like Fort Knox, the courtyard, forty pounds deeper from eight months of daily one hundred wide-arm pull ups. Read enough books to wallpaper my old eight-by-five cell, wait till the two-three-four boys, The Courtyard Saints, and Lily see the new me.

So boom, right, I head outside and hit the middle entrance of the courtyard. Hoping for someone in the past to walk by so I can drop some fresh knowledge. You know everybody needs a gem or two. Anything more than that is going to run you two cans of octopus and a bag of rice and beans. So boom, check it. One of my co-defendants, Windog, passes by and asks me how's everything and "I'm like, I'm comprehending, I'm comprehending, you know knowledge of self." He starts looking at me strange like,

"Word, um . . . yeah, you look like you put on some weight."

And I'm like, "there is a necessity for it."

"O . . . k . . . Did you learn your lesson?"

"It's not what I learned, it's what I gained. See, I am a mirror image of the generation that is to come. I did everything looking for acceptance. 'Cause I didn't have acceptance at home. It's ostentatious. Win looks at me like,

"Homie, you are six away from a six-pack. Hey, isn't that your girl across the street?"

I'm like, "Nah my brother. I'm thinking right now in the immediate."

THERE'S a familiar smell in the air
designer imposter perfume
mixed with the cooked smell
of Just For Me hair relaxer
always equals Lily
there she go
my first day out
and she is across the street

in the arms of a rival
one of my enemies
from the fifth-ave boys
her skirt raised half a foot higher
than when I left her
her hair dyed a red manic panic.

"Picture me going back to selling drugs, Win. That's insidious." He says to me,

"Dog, you turned crazy."

"I'm like, yeah, it's a possibility, but not a probability. You can't go from Guatemala to guatepeor. See, but what I learned is that Picasso lives amongst us. He's just in prison, being deprived of his expression and deprivation. That's why crime doesn't pay. Now all I need is a job."

'95

I guess all the sophisticatededed talk intimidates the J-O-Bs from employing me. Or maybe it is the square box on the dozen-fold of applications that I sell myself short to for not lying when they ask, "Have you ever been convicted of a Felony? If so, please check." The worst is when they lay out the horizontal line followed by the horizontal question, "If you have been convicted, please describe the crime." And just like the American way, honesty will get you nowhere. Summer of '95, so tough on my spirit, I lie down on the tar beach of my roof for hours wishing, wondering, why life can't be like a Shaolin Wallabe. You know, blue and cream? Why does the everyday struggle swallow so hard like I'm drinking liquid swords? I dig knee-deep into my pockets and there is not a single dead president to represent me.

That summer of '95, one thousand degrees in the shade, if it isn't the Babazi that got me wide, it's the liqs baby, the liqs, to numb it all away. But sparking mad 'izm, tapping the bottle and twisting the cap doesn't always make things feel funk-doobiest. Too much of it fries my brain enough to electrocute a barracuda. So with the last big L lit, I crush, kill, destroy the stress of UPS not hiring me and decide to sell crack again, decide to give the wicked jump shot of slanging rocks one more chance, though this time it's gotta be B-I-G big. This time I'm gonna get this dough or die. So I judge wisely, as if nothing ever surprises me, and decide to chase these rumors of nicks going for twenties down south. Midwestern money creeping on a come-up.

So the fab five of us Courtyard Saints deal-in. It's me, Bein, and the other three ask me to hide their identity, so for now we will call them Le Flow, Le Fla, Eshkoshka. We grab ourselves a local moyo with some Midwestern roots, cut him in on the deal, and us skull rag wearing prospectors hit that Autumn Road. Heading out to Franklin County, Ohio, on the Greyhound bus. Body-n-bags strapped with Saran-Wrapped balls of one hundred vial cracks shaped into eight-sided dice. Each of us assigned a different firearm in case there is a pit stop called the police. I look in my Jansport bag to see the lead shooter I am unlicensed to serve and it is the gun John Wayne couldn't even stand the reign of, the TEC-9. Every state line we cross is a new charge. Every

LEMON ANDERSEN

89

bullet in the chamber adds an extra year, which totals life. But I can't be shook, 'cause there is no such thing as a half-way crook.

———

WE OUTTA
TOWN

WE outta town, so sunny bright
getting it, doubled money plight
right here they crack smiles
but ain't a damn thing funny, right

We outta town, thoroughbound
no bodegas all around
no local trains found
ain't prepped to how it's going down

We outta town, ain't the only ones
everyone got guns
Courtyard Saints on this run
twisted
came out here to have fun

We outta town grown

unknown
all alone
kid named Mookie
sees us on our own
tells us
we can have these streets sown

We outta town
paranoia
by this new gutter
talking 'bout, they miss they girls
talking 'bout, they miss they mothers
M double-O
K
Mookie
look he
walks in
and he's one mad brother
he says . . .

Franklin
COUNTY

"FUCK Jay-Z man, I don't bel'ee that New York hype no more man. Look at you big city boys packing, getting ready to go back home. You pushers ain't got no heart. When I first saw you all last week at Rally's eating a Big Buford burger I says to myself, I know y'all were not from our side of town cause y'all keep calling each other son and B' and we don't be getting down like that on this side of the road, you feel me. So I put you goons up at my sister Tonya's spot nears Censored, I calls it Censored cause y'all don't need to know where the fucks she be'ez at. I got y'all a crib where y'all can move them goods and double up and y'all is fienin' to go back home, talking 'bout you miss your mommas. Fuck that, out here we think like this, M.O.B— money over bitches, even if it's your momma, 'cause she be the first one to ask if she could hold something. What happened to all that New York thugness? What happened to live from Bedford-Stuyvesant? What, you thought Columbus, Ohio, don't spill blood? That's an hourly thang out here man, but y'all should be used to that, since y'all be soapbox preaching that gangster shit all day in your songs. Talking 'bout represent, represent, and not one of you folks is fienin' to represent, hold it down out here, and make this money, son, B."

"Hey Mook?"

"What, what it do Lemonhead?"

"Why don't you chill, before one of us slaps your ass with a tate quieto stick. Now, I'm down to ride 'cause I came out here to make this money, so go back to your lil' '74 Impala with them tin foil ass rims and wait for me, I will be right wit'cha."

"Ya see, that's what the fuck I'm talking 'bout, nah, you ain't Lemonhead to me no more cuz, you just Lemon, 'cuz there ain't nothing sweet about a lemon. I'ma be out in the car waitin' for you, rolling you up some of this good green fo' sho', bumping that new Bone Thugz. The rest of you are a bunch of mark-ass busters."

"Hey, don't listen to that dude. Y'all go back home where love is love. I'ma stay out here and finish what we came here to do. There ain't nothing for me back home anyway."

For the next week, while my boys are back in the courtyard with their families playing the saint, I'm down in Columbus, Ohio, riding shot gun with Mook down alleys, selling crack on picket fence porches, partying in parking lots. They even celebrate Halloween two days early out here and call it "Beggar's Day" so the kids don't get killed before the first of the month. It's a Midwestern thing.

Day before the first of the month, Mookie takes me to a Monday night football game. During halftime a squad of strippers come out in cat suits, devil thongs, butterfly wings. They turned the second half of that game into a stripper masquerade party.

So after the French maid christens me with a lap dance, Mook drives me over to the crack house. I start telling him how much fun I'm having,

> "Hey Mook, I ain't never even spoke much before now I know this, I just been all about making this money. I didn't know what to expect when I came out here, man. Doesn't feel any different from where I came from, at least how I came up. See, that's what makes me different from them fools I was rolling with. That's why I can hang in this here Columbus, 'cause I ain't ghetto, I'm poor like you and everybody else out here."

"Damn, that's some deep shit Lemon. You fucking with my high. You one of the homies, Lemon. You know what I'm fienin' to do? I'm fienin' to send you a crackhead to go give you some head at the crack house. Hey, Lorraine, c'mere shawty, ya see this dude right here, this is my dude. Here's some ready-roc, go in there and suck the kids out of him. See, now that's how you take care of the homie."

[THE]
RAID

WELCOME to the best suck off I ever got in my life
Play that horn like a bugle boy baby
Don't stop till you hit that last note
Welcome to more money in my pocket
Her head rested on my lap
A toothless ecstasy, I am so . . .

Welcome, please don't stop, baby
She tells me,
"Last person who
called me baby, took away my smile."

Welcome to the fiends lined up outside
Waiting for the mailman to be
Their deliverer, so I can serve them
Their savior
And I will

No matter how much it hurts my mother's
Spirit to see me like this

Welcome to the birds

[chirp]

The static radio

[chirp]

What was that?

[chirp]

Nah baby, don't stop

[chirp]
[static]
[static chirp]

The raid
The sawed-off shotgun blown to the back of the head . . .
    blunt
Lights out
The raid

[static]

[static chirp]

Ammonia
The raid
I know that smell
The raid

Ammonia
It's the Polo cologne of all institutions
The raid

Ammonia
Handcuffed to a bed
Hospitals don't have tomato-face sheriffs
Schools don't have part-time wardens
But they all smell the same

Ammonia

"Eat what you are served, boy."
"Never speak up when you are spoken down to."

This sure ain't Riker's Island.

ATTICA,
ATTICA,
ATTICA

WELCOME to Ohio Franklin County Jail
it makes Sing Sing Maximum look Trump upscale
one shower, one toilet, thirty-five males
no outside rec, no bones to inhale
no views of the sun
the blacks are all pale
serving pork to kosher Muslims
bread is all stale
if this was Attica, Attica, Attica
then we would raise hell

Prison privatization got us all for sale
all you got is your word
your orange jumpsuit
your uncertified mail
even the officer female
with her Press-On Lee nails

telling us that we fail
but she's locked up too
she just calls it a job detail
she don't know that with a hunger strike
we can rise and prevail
against diabetic sugar-based commissary
sold to us in retail
Attica, Attica, Attica

Your current affair
I know you weren't aware
that we're in the pen
y'all need to live for yourself
instead you living on a prayer
be aware, but don't beware
care, but don't be scared
prepare to compare
fair with the unfair
don't ever let no one, no how
tell you, you not a man
live with regret for what you did
but keep the same heart
that put that crime in your hand
fight for your right to at least
breathe democratica
and if they don't give us that human right
then we give them
Attica, Attica, Attica

IT WAS
WRITTEN...

"A future indictment for Andersen."

Yells the officer at the gate, which means they're letting me loose 'cause the Ohio county jails are too packed, and some of us have to walk the plank. I trade in my orange jumpsuit for that small-town Ohio sky which kicks cold like a Buckeye. I see Mook and sell my trendy clothes to him for a Greyhound bus ticket and leave some mix tapes in his car for him to ride to.

"I gotta go back home, but I don't know what I'm going home to, but I know the world is not a ghetto. The only difference between us and the privileged is that they're just a step ahead. All we gotta do is double up."

The next fifteen-hour ride back home goes blackout. It stares down at me like Fort Knox. I'm back in Brooklyn staring at the courtyard with a military bag in hand, outstayed my welcome at my boy Lou da Barber's, and fixed on living a new life, even if it means living on the street. The Courtyard Saints is no longer my dig.

The next morning I wake up on a hard furnished room floor in the Cleveland and Essex section of East New York. Time cooped up between call girls and baby mothers, my brother Peter barely stays here. He just passes by to drop off the key and some money for me to cut my hair and look decent for a job search.

The local fade shop has its own history of clients who use it as a hangout and a gossip corner, which means I have to settle for the weakest barber who pays his chair rental from cutting walk-ins. All the barbers happen to be named José, so how they are separated is by nicknames like Fat José, Skinny José, Pimple José, and Dick-nose. And their argument is who's the best MC: Biggie, Jay-Z, or Nas. During their rap state debate, a Woodstock high school girl with a hip-hop mullet walks in handing out flyers for a poetry reading tonight going down in the south side of Williamsburg at a community center called El Puente. The fee to get in is a five-spot and all I have is ten for a cut, but I'm a victim of KRS-One. Knowledge reigns supreme over nearly everybody, so instead I get a lineup for five, hop that J train to Marcy Ave looking forward to hearing people read their poems. I reach El Puente and it looks like the church precinct from *21 Jumpstreet*. I walk in and I'm greeted with love and a quick pat down. Chairs are being lined up for congregation. Canvas Taino art and student picket signs are nailed to the wall for ambiance. The host, newly published, about the flyest Palestinian phoenix I have ever seen. Her face all-too-familiar, like she was once a Sunset Park Arab. She calls up each poet personally, like they are related to her, and one by one every voice seems to be in a league of its own.

The
Poets

MuMs da Schemer and his tale of the confident cock-roach. Nymflow 9 uses the anatomy of a *Dr. Giggles* surgeon to tell his love poems in dark tone. Tkalla crumps, clowns, dances around the mic stand without losing breath or story arc. DJ Cucumber Slice, a.k.a. Bobbito, a.k.a. Kool Bob Love passionately laughs about sneakers and donuts. Bonafide holds on to the last cry of the Young Lords. Sonya Renee sweet-talks the Black Arts Movement into your ear.

All this rhythm and rhyme without a single break beat to use as an audible. Then the Palestinian phoenix options the open mic list being full to the crowd and for the first time in my life I feel I have something to say, the fly way. I beg the host to give me a shot, hear me roar, and when she turns to look at me her eyes shine with mama Africa. She says,

*"Honey, the list is closed, but give me your
name and be ready stage left if I call you."*

There is one problem, I don't have a poem, but I do have
an experience. Now, if I can creatively control it, it might
just land on the ear one time. Near me is this fax machine
with blank copy paper stuck in it. I take a couple of sheets
and lose myself on my people, places, and things. My name
is called out through the rented speakers right on the last
line, perfect like an Olympic dismount. I walk to the stage
and cop a rookie artist's plea.

"My name is Lemon and there's nothing sweet about what
I got to say . . ."

The
Poem

THIS is a toast to freedom
just 'cause you're locked up
don't mean you can't be free
matter of fact, the first day of your bid
the options are available
the doors wide open

You can be Muslim
and sing a song to raise the sun
You can be a Five-Percenter
and understand that the mathematics behind the lan-
    guage of
Kemetics is that it is the original tongue of man, my
    brother
You can be Christian
and go from being Catholic to being confused
to knowing the only way is to fear God

and you got nothing to lose
everything to gain
Can I get a witness?
"Amen"
You can be a Nazi and hate all of the above
but we don't get much of those round here
plus, the Israelites will set that ass straight
But you got to believe in something
or you will be a rhythmless void

So here's a toast to my God
and all of y'all who play the yard
may your word be born and may you find
that the Lord may not come when you call
but he's always on time

GLORY

I thought about how they all listened, not to the words in my mind, they listened to the talent of my heart. Big words don't define passion. A Yoruba lady who read a poem about her left breast approaches me in the spotlight of my life and asks me about how would I feel doing community service, and before I could say, "For what, hopping the train?" She sells me a job opportunity working in her theater troupe. I really don't hear theatre more than I hear the word "job." I mean, I never been offered one, and by this point begged for too many. She puts her business card in my clammy stage-frightened hand and bids me a good night.

I jump that Marcy Ave. train fare and three hipsters greet

me to a round of applause. I treat them to a moment of stardom and give them a humble nod like glory is nothing new to me. But it is. It's the first time I taste anything priceless. I walk to the end of the platform where the fearless wait for the train and face the pimp Godot, who is sitting wide-legged on the top of the Williamsburg Bridge, and push his ass to the side to tell . . .

My mother you can sleep now fall back for I have found my calling, my beacon. Just watch me carjack a sonnet in thirty-five seconds tops, make the holidays in the hood holy again. Watch me make the crowds tighten their cipher, make black folks give my two-step this get out of town look. Millie just remember to tell 'em when they ask who bore that child remember to tell them,

"That's My Boy!"

GLOSSARY

B'	Short for boy or homeboy.
BCW	Acronym for Bureau of Child Welfare.
BE'LEE	Phonetic variation of believe.
BOMBIN'	To tag up or paint graffiti on a wall or other surface in a public area.
BOOGIE Down	Term that refers to Bronx, New York.
BOP	An exaggerated form of walking.
BUCK-FIFTY	A deep cut across a person's face usually from the temple to the corner of the mouth. Derives from the myth that it takes one-hundred and fifty stitches to close the wound.
CHEEZIN'	Term that means to smile with enthusiasm.
DAT'S	Phonetic variation of that's.
DEF	Term used to describe a person, place, thing, or event that is cool.

DEUCE-DEUCE	A small caliber handgun.
DOI	A variation of duh.
FLAT-BLACK	A type of finish for paint colors.
FIVE-PERCENT NATION	An offshoot of the Nation of Islam, leaders and members consider themselves to be the poor righteous teachers. The five-percent of the population that is enlightened, and has knowledge of self.
FIVE-PERCENTER	A poor righteous teacher. A member of the Five-Percent Nation.
GEE	Term meaning gangsta or guy.
GOONIE	A variation of goon. A reference to a group of characters of the movie *The Goonies*.
GRAFF	Short for graffiti.
JOU	Phonetic variation of you.
JOUR	Phonetic variation of your.
HUEVO Boots	Knee-high boots, that gather at the ankle.
I'MA	Short for "I'm going to . . ."
IZM	Another term for marijuana.
L	Marijuana rolled in cigar leafs.
LQS	Short for Latin Quarters, a popular dance club in New York City.
LIQS	Another term for liquor.
LUMBERJACK	A type of jacket.
MARK-ASS	A victim or target of a scheme; a sucker or patsy.
MC	Master of Ceremony; rapper.

Meng	Phonetic variation of man.
Nicks	A bag of weed that costs five dollars.
Pizoem	Phonetic variation of poem.
Prenda Lady	A lady from the neighborhood who sells jewelry.
PT	Acronym for physical training.
Ready-roc	Another term for crack.
Rec	Short for recreation.
Shaped-up	Also known as a line-up. Done by trimming the outer most edges of the hairline.
Shawty	Variation of shorty; a female.
Six-step	A break dancing move.
South Boogie Down	Another term for the neighborhood known as the South Bronx in New York City.
Sophisticatededed	Phonetic variation of sophisticated.
Spoken-word	Term used to describe performance poetry.
Syringey	A phonetic variation of the word syringe.
Two-step	A type of dance.
Vewy	Phonetic variation of very.
Wack-ass	A lame or sorry ass person.
Whaddup	Phonetic variation of what's up?
Wit' Cha	Phonetic variation of with you.

NOTES

Que tu cre'?	**What do you think?**
Que el problema?	**What's the problem?**
Tu si que jode	**You bother a lot**
Porque	**Because**
Juntos me vuelven a la super condenao loca	**Together you two drive me super crazy**
Yo fui a el	**I went to the**
Los pelos de los panties mi'jo	**The hairs from my underwear**
En el	**In the**
Quedáte con tu pai'	**Stay with you father**
Blanco desgraciao concho	**Disgraceful white man**
Campo	**The country**
Prenda	**Jewelry**
Pero	**But**
Tetas	**Breasts**
Pegao	**The cooked rice stuck at the bottom of the pot**

Sancocho	**Stew**
Novelas	**Soap operas**
Si	**Yes**
Mira	**Look**
Por mi	**For me**
Mi'jo	**My son**
La familia	**The family**
Eyo creen que la SIDA e un denomio	**They think that AIDS is a demon**
Cuando yo me muero	**When I die don't**
No te pone como los puertoriqueños	**Act like those Puerto Ricans**
Tu y las palabras	**You and your words**
Oye me	**Listen to me**
Los dia van hacer malo	**There are days that are going to be bad**
E' mucho para ti	**Is too much for you**
Y mi enfermedad te cay mal	**And my illness is hard on you**
Aguantate *Lucha para tu paz*	**Hold on to yourself** **Fight for your peace**
Porque cuando yo no estoy aqui mas na	**Because when I'm no longer here**
So no te pones como un cabronsito	**Don't act like at little bastard**
Que tu eres un nene bueno	**That you are a good boy**

Las gentes	**The people**
Y algo mas	**And one more thing**
No vas a funeraria mia	**Don't go to my funeral**
Me entiendes	**You understand me**
Quinceñera	**Like sweet sixteen only on a girl's fifteenth birthday**
Tu quiere un party?	**You want a party?**
Metete e'te deo y hacete un party con eso	**Here's me middle finger throw a party with that**

LEMON ANDERSEN is a critically acclaimed renaissance artist. He has the greatest number of appearances on HBO's *Russell Simmons Presents Def Poetry*, with eight performances in six seasons. Lemon is an original cast member of *Russell Simmons' Def Poetry Jam on Broadway*. The show took home the Tony Award for "Special Theatrical Event" in 2003 and the Drama Desk nomination for "Unique Theatrical Experience." Lemon has been a pioneer in the spoken-word and theater scene for the past decade, performing at venues such as the Apollo Theater, The Chicago Theater, Hollywood's Kodak Theater and The Nuyorican Poets Cafe. Lemon's screen actor and writing credits include *The Soloist*, starring Robert Downey Jr. and Jamie Foxx, as well as Spike Lee's *Miracle At St. Anna, Sucker Free City, She Hate Me*, and he appeared opposite Denzel Washington in *Inside Man*. His theater credits include the Jo Bonney directed *Slanguage*, which premiered at the New York Theater Workshop to rave reviews and sold out shows. Lemon has taught performance art workshops at both colleges and correctional facilities, from the University of Michigan, to New York's infamous Sing Sing prison, to Harvard University. He has studied master acting with Wynn Handman at Carnegie Hall and delved into Shakespeare at the Public Lab.

Lemon is the author of *Ready Made Real*, a collection of original poems. He is currently touring *County of Kings*, his staged memoir which was produced by Spike Lee and the Culture Project and premiered at the Public Theater. The book based on the show was the Grand Prize Winner of the 2010 New York Book Festival. His poetry has been featured on everything from radio and viral spots, to print ads, and most recently on the limited edition Absolut Brooklyn bottle. A native New Yorker, Lemon currently resides in Brooklyn with is wife and daughters.